Sacrum

Also by Bruce Bond:

Prose:
Immanent Distance: Poetry and the Metaphysics of the Near at Hand (2015)

Poetry:
Gold Bee (2016)
Black Anthem (2016)
For the Lost Cathedral (2015)
The Other Sky (2015)
Choir of the Wells: A Tetralogy (2013)
The Visible (2012)
Peal (2009)
Blind Rain (2008)
Cinder (2003)
The Throats of Narcissus (2001)
Radiography (1997)
The Anteroom of Paradise (1991)
Independence Days (1990)

Sacrum

Bruce Bond

Four Way Books
Tribeca

Please direct all inquiries to:
Editorial Office
Four Way Books
POB 535, Village Station
New York, NY 10014
www.fourwaybooks.com

Library of Congress Cataloging-in-Publication Data

Names: Ossmann, April, author.
Title: Event boundaries / April Ossmann.
Description: New York, NY : Four Way Books, [2017]
Identifiers: LCCN 2016034897 | ISBN 9781935536857 (pbk. : alk. paper)
Classification: LCC PS3615.S634 A6 2017 | DDC 811/.6--dc23
LC record available at https://lccn.loc.gov/2016034897

This book is manufactured in the United States of America and printed on acid-free paper.

Four Way Books is a not-for-profit literary press. We are grateful for the assistance we receive from individual donors, public arts agencies, and private foundations.

This publication is made possible with public funds from the New York State Council on the Arts, a state agency.

We are a proud member of the Community of Literary Magazines and Presses.

Distributed by University Press of New England
One Court Street, Lebanon, NH 03766

Contents

III.

"Heal the sick" means —help them regain their lost unity without depriving them of their abundance.

—Paul Tillich

I.

Snow

In Memory of Jack Myers

I am calling out to you where you sleep
off the rest of our night,
our chill, our little century,
where snow falls as it has never fallen,
not here, not with the weight
of hours that drug these oaks,
that break our dark umbrella at the stem.
All day the great book of heaven
plunges through the shredder—
the book of life, you called it,
not sure who or what life
noted there, if living was alone
the afterworld of books. No birds.
No traffic. None to speak of.
Just an engine now and then,
a tattered flag of smoke, dissolving.
I am calling out to you, I say,
though you were always one
to speak for the quiet of days
like this, for the straight talk
with just so many feathers on its arrow.
Not that quiet comes easily.
Far from it. Or that we live to hear it
beat our pillows where we lie.
Is it true, morning presses us to seek
what never arrives, not comfort
merely, but the voice inside
the voice, yours in particular,
inside the print, the page,

the winter field. Even the body
of someone I love, someone I trust
to be there when I wake,
is one of those blizzards I walk
into, head down, eyes blinded.
Surely tonight the heavens are on fire.
I know this the way I know the birds
exist, that they take their songs,
their need for songs, into some
white space at the heart of winter,
heads tucked beneath their wings.
I know this the way a child knows
the sweetness of words she cannot
understand, and it is this knowledge
that leads to understanding.
I know this the way happiness knows
something I do not, the way
a body knows its machinery
of breath that fits into the world.
Just think of the mourner
who stood before the TV with you inside it,
how he paused to warm his face
by the fire. Even in grief
we pour out word after word
to make room for more.
Contentment is the art that wears its art
lightly. You taught me that.
Perhaps that's because you broke it
open like a marriage, tinkered

at the inner workings late, until,
speechless, beat, pale as dawn, you collapsed
into dream. I know: sleep is not easy.
Still I want to find you there.
I want to believe this quiet when it says
joy is not its own grave,
that what I see when I think of you
is snow, the blizzard of a lifetime.
This day without you
blazing through your body as it falls.

Heart Murmur

It begins the way all language begins,
in the dark web of nerves that touch the skin
of those who, skinless, would unnerve us.
Just what it says is anyone's guess:
a wing clipped, a valve in stutters, blood
in the fabric we tend to take for granted.
If it were clear, it would be as silent
as an eye. Or the lantern hung inside it.
But we are well below the throat now,
between the tongue and the pain it swallows.
The body, when it breaks a little, opens
something. What we need needs us. Listen,
says the hall of clocks, the drunken hour,
that stumbles, turns, and walks a little more.

Blood

When I was a boy, I believed the science
that said life on earth began in the sea,

and when it crawled ashore it took a little
of the ocean with it, its blood composed

of the same salt and minerals that gave
the tide its metal. And I believed despite

the more obvious questions: just how
the vital water turned the color of wine,

what it was that washed us to the shore,
unconscious, a child of the child we were.

When I laid my ear against the pillow,
I heard it: the thump and shush of waves

against some beach in the bedroom dark,
and in the moment of my strange reunion,

I felt alone, the way the dead must feel
as they walk across their stretch of ocean

barely touching down. This is my blood,
read the men in black from a black book.

Drink. It was one of those things we did
because, like them, we wanted to belong.

If this was the sea, it had traveled far,
from cloud to grape, to the body's faith

in those who shared fears they barely spoke of.
Unresolvable and vast. Like water.

Unruly until it chills the shape of something.
Brine is poison to us now. Not wine.

I have a friend whose wine was poison.
I drink it in memory. And then I stop.

Grief can kill you, and who can live without
crossing the many oceans each night to find

a language for the exclusions of the day.
Out of the sea, we came, bearing with us

its changing weather, its need to change, to *feed*.
I love that word. The give in it that takes.

Water to wine to blood, each one spilling
into one like some death wish at the heart

of love. This is my body, says the sea.
Eat. I will never be the friend I carry

like an ocean on my back, never the blood
he drank and never the same. If the sea

in the fierceness of its solitude
takes us in, if there are moments the crumpling

of the waves is quieter than silence,
is it any wonder we return. Like blood.

When I was a boy, I had an enormous
space in me. It might have been the future

or past, I could not tell, but it was larger
than the flesh that bore it. Larger than life

or death or the ocean path between them.
When those I loved left, their names came back.

They found us. They floated their empty boats
from breath to breath I barely knew was there.

Consolation

The hospital café plays soprano sax
in the loose-limbed unconflicted style
of cheer floating through the night-light.
Most of us sit alone with our phones
and talk, if we talk, to no one here.
Trays, when abandoned, wait for hours
with their half-carved cubes of lemon jello,
the scraps of meat that were just too much,
or not enough of something else, and so
would not go down. The music understands
this is no place to add to the burden,
though the soft rock and Kenny G of denial
lifts no heart I know. Still, it knows
something about being left behind,
and so becomes the dull and loyal friend
our problems tend to take for granted.
It hums its air conditioner hum,
waiting for that thing to happen, that news
to break and so to break us. It knows
the confusion of the tongue dumbed
with novocaine, fumbling the words,
or the woman in the lobby who watches
the surgeon come in, sit down, and talk,
his mask pulled down and gathered at his throat.
She watches his lips. They are deliberate.
They are slow. And more cold than ever,
the music goes swiftly through her now,
without dissidence, blood, or cruel surprise.

Nostalgia for the Infinite

There are more enigmas in the shadow of a man who walks in the sun than in all the religions of the past, present and future.

—Giorgio de Chirico

As a child once, as he alone kept
vigil over his sleeping father,
he watched the moon lay a fever

on the town, equally asleep,
as were his mother and brother,
waiting out the long departure.

The nightingales that poured their
voices through the window were,
to him, one nightingale, one song.

The small party in the distance,
the sound of a guitar, a woman's
laugh—they too owed their luster

to the dark world that held them
to each other, like stars that pin
the long threads of gods between them.

And so he walked, left the others
to their solitudes and took in
something of the feathered night

that, mercifully, knew nothing.
Like some dream that goes under
as the dreamer rises, showers,

ties his shoes. The loneliness
of trains and banners, of the spare
and towered architecture calls

a body to its shadow, a shadow
to the amber of open spaces.
There are reasons a boy walks

without a place in mind, the moon
floating a silhouette behind him.
Reasons we bury the dead in smoke

and dirt and see them in between.
Is there no beauty without distance,
he asks. No moonlight but the sun.

People say our first ancestral
work of art was the outline
of a shadow. Like a first word.

There are reasons we too walk
our shadows on our leashes
long after they have vanished.

What we do know is the boy
returned. And he sketched his father
who died soon after the sketch was done.

Just a head. No room. No wall.
And when the boy slept at last,
he was neither outdoors nor in.

But both. Not a boy alone
but always in some future place
he would never leave again.

Hourglass

In my house no one ever died. They *passed away*
into the whispered sympathy of a father's voice,

the way he knelt to admit some difficult news,
to make known facts he was powerless to explain.

It felt kinder, to offer the dead a measure of calm
designed to comfort the living, to break our fall

against the give of the departed. However still
the heart, the something there continued to move.

Away he said, never to presume arrival,
only this ache of passage, the gravity of marble,

the date that stamps each marker like a passport.
And though my father gave us one kind of silence,

we heard another in translation. Tough to say
how much was reverence, how much the raw place

he bound in something soft. The father in him
was just him now, left to shadow the last arrangements.

Work never ends because, he knew, it always ends.
You could see it in his look, the numbered hours

that bent his body to the page, the night's one lamp
with its veil of light, motionless and burning.

Déjà Vu

Perhaps it is our longing
to see the part that sees,
coaxed out from its place
of hiding, like the shadow
page you soon will turn
to lay upon another.
Perhaps there is a bone
to mend, a heart we hardened
when we were far away.
The past is always out there—
we know that—and never is.
Forgiveness is difficult
for this reason. And sweet.
You see it everywhere,
the dead hand that brought you
into the world, the birth
cry you cannot remember.
Somewhere a wasp unzips
the air and we pass through.
No, you have never passed
this way before. And yet
this particular spoon,
with the ceiling fan
spinning in its eye,
is on the verge of something,
confessing its attachment,
taking you, like some
drunk exaggeration, back.
Try, it says, to feed

yourself in both worlds,
to give to both, fit in,
and so move about more
freely. As if we might
forget when we are
thinking of forgetting.
Or look a little closer
by looking at the act
of looking. We might, you know.
Try, say all the fathers
with their dying and ours,
to blaze without burning,
the way one sun blazes
with many suns, and none
so blinding as today.

May 3rd

When her husband's diagnosis came,
she broke into two people, one who watched

the other watch him say, *I've had a good life,*
and then say nothing. And say it again.

And as the weeks brought with them the quiet
waiting rooms alone, the seasonal rains

reminded her of other Mays, when tragedy
split the third day of the month in two:

a death, a stroke, and now this, May 3rd
the random needle that stitches them together.

Misery loves a needle. It loves to slip
a thread through eye of the storm and pull.

And she repeated the numbers in her head—
5/3—as if they were the combination

to some locker at the end of the world.
And in that locker, a tiny phonograph

that made the kind of sense that music makes
as it returns to the opening theme,

surprised, inevitably, its voice a half-step
closer to God and never coming down.

Hackberry

I never could find them, my cat's bones,
though I know still they are somewhere near,

laid beneath the hackberry we cut down
to make room for the study we are building.

I have tried, thinking less about my cat's
attachments than my wife's, the unearthed grief

that wanders our yard, looking for the new
resting place and trees to give it shade.

These days are long, and the parts we play
lie down long before our bodies follow,

so when she saw the tree taken from what
was once our plan to take it, the loss seemed

more clear and thus more difficult to see.
I tried. And so broke ground like a promise

around the holes that soon would turn to anchors,
buckets of concrete to pin our floorboards down.

I loved that cat the way a room loves a door
that turns to sky each time it opens. Once

we held her high and said that she was flying,
pretended too to catch her purring body

which we talked to constantly, pretending.
She taught me, love is not quite empathy,

however strong those roots in us, not quite
what animal grace may or may not know.

I never could find her, nor the broken doll
that is her body, though I swore I stood there,

and kept digging where I just was until
everything went soft. Forgive me, cat, you

who lie down in the wife who lies in me
so deep no spade can find you. Hard for us

to tell sometimes. Was it pleasure or sleep
that closed your eyes. Was it you who flew.

The Falling Sickness

Once it was a sign
gods had taken over

and plunged the captive spirit
deep into the well

of the body, there,
where light is just a word.

Or so said the well
none could fathom, not even

the man with his bones
in shivers, eyes seized,

gazing so far upward
his pupils disappeared.

Just what he hoped to see
no one knew. No one

looked as hard, as far
as he, or ached for days

with the afflatus of men's
bewildered admiration.

He who passeth over
death's river and back.

It frightened all of them,
the faceless thing beneath

a face, the place without
form that gripped the form

we give. To suffer this
was to walk in two worlds,

exiled to a heaven
that does not hear you.

And even if it could,
what sense would it make.

What peace would you broker
with your bitten tongue.

Your unfamiliar language
a god's, a body's, who's

to say. One world says,
we do not have bodies.

We *are* them. The other
whispers, *fall*. And we fall.

Glossolalia

After the fall, when my father struck his head
and staggered into months of sleep,

we kept vigil with words
traded softly across his bed, not knowing

what it was he heard, let alone understood,
or if he closed the dry wound behind him as he slept.

Still we greeted him with a flock of hands
as if he were a garden statue

who wore the wings of an unfamiliar day.
The green light clipped to his index finger

took the pulse inside it—*to take,*
the way a thief takes the jewel he needs

to stay alive. It takes distance to read
most anything, to make it ours.

*

I want to believe the music when it says,
there is another world, an earth

so close none can see it. There is a language
that speaks before we speak.

And what, I ask, of the speech before that,
and so on. What of the infant

who hears in songs her father sings
the word her future self will choose.

Where does her babble end, the world begin.

*

Say you wake from the long dream of forgotten life,
if only to speak a foreign English,

a broken tongue full of stutters and exasperations.
You too might wonder at the failure

of others to see, to hear. I want to trust
my father's eyes, the way a reader of wells

trusts the oracle inside them, the star
that gems each dark descending throat.

To say he is in there somewhere
suggests he has the power to know,

to wear the black a miner wears, pinned
in the rubble of his own strange flesh.

Always a language before the language,
but whose.

*

Ask any grieving mother if there is no end
to interpretation: death is a word

that cuts the bread of the world. It lies down
in beds of stone. What is more certain

than the cloak we drape across the mirror.
It is the bridge that arcs into the fog

that will not lift. Perhaps you too have felt it,
staring off hours on end, when you start to see

the birth of every language drawn up
out of the brine, a giant cloud dripping with sleep.

Perhaps you hear the speaker inside the speaker,
and so on, until the self dissolves

against the ocean mist. Like salt.

*

It took Charles Berlitz years to remember
what it was like, growing up, each person in his clan

addressing him in a different language:
his father German, his grandfather Russian,

his nanny Spanish, and so on. He understood
this as the way life was and would be,

each word indiscernible from the hand that wrote it.
And though the many tongues clarified on his,

eight in all, every one a mother tongue,
though he turned to each kind face to part

the darkness in it, he wondered why
he did not have a language of his own.

*

I have never known the charisma that speaks
in tongues, the speech of fire, they call it,

as if the will to make a new language, a cant
of sparks, consumed something of the man who speaks it.

Brains tell us there are flames beneath these temples
that talk. They say to speak in tongues

requires a place in the mind far
from other conversations. Is all our language

the language of faith. Not a child's faith merely,
borne out of nothing into a pool of sunlight,

our first word ours alone and always.
Is all our language the company we keep

reinventing, the speaker and the spoken
a family of one.

*

Once I sat beside my father on a bench that watched
the turning pages of the bay and asked him

for the stories I barely understood,
though I imagined a region beneath his damaged speech,

a day not unlike the one before us,
an ocean park where the grass was hair

and everything shimmered.
Sky plunged into the sky. It's how I cope:

making up the parts he could not know
he carried to his grave. No end

to the man beneath the man, and so on.
And as I helped him from our vigil to the car,

my hand his crutch, the feathered sound
of waves against our backs, I watched my every step,

and his. Like walking on fire.
All language the language of things

we give our lives to say.

Mouth

Once you cupped the wick
lit with a surge of milk,
and as you grew, hunger
grew, and as you sighed,
made large by desires
that made me small, the *O*
from which I first drank
bound me to its absence.
Even now I go weak
against the warmth of bodies
that are not there, and yet
I relish my appetite
for what it cannot fill,
how it, like blood, persists,
less as meaningful
than filled with the purpose
meaning longs to possess.
If only I could cut light
into small and smaller
morsels. To speak this way
showers me with pins
and angels beyond number.
The archer knows, poised
to split the sweet spot:
the tinier the better,
the deeper the attraction
that focuses the needle.

Sweet red dwarf star, sweet heart
of the target, sweet pistil
of the rose whose petals
ripple outward. Like a cry.

II.

Belladonna

Those who pinched the tincture of nightshade
in their eyes, who saw in them the blades

of darker blooms it takes the dark to see,
how could they know the distillate of leaves

that bruised their pupils with the clear seed
would, in its blossoming, make them blind.

Or, if not blind, then incoherent, immune
to the pain of things that would define them.

Now we know. Two berries could put an end
to you, but one, and your hand begins

to take on the chill of the drinking glass,
before you lose all sense of hands and glasses.

This too is how to resurrect a world
you took for granted, to hold what you once held,

how it shaped the bones you did not know
you moved, until the belladonna showed you.

Poison, yes, but an ally of the surgeon
back when folks were desperate to be numb.

Companion too of the pleasure seeker
who longed to bring some misery to flower,

to rival the uneasiness of being.
And who can blame him, haloed in the bees

of amazement, less at what he touched
than what he will not, cannot, the dull triumph

of mind over matters. Or so it seemed.
There, there, says the north wind as it leaves,

and it keeps saying it. Like the phantom
limb that aches vaguely now and then.

The glories of the field turn the blood
and rust shades of the long-in-closing wound,

and who can fault us if we break the stems
to lay across the bronzes and their names.

Everywhere you look, the slow-to-mend,
the battlefield whose blossoms now are legend.

Hymnals rise to take us somewhere far
from the horrible arrangement, our stranger

boxed in rouge and candles on the dais,
our kiss withheld the moment we get close.

What we draw back breaks us slowly down,
as cold breaks down the puzzle of the fall.

The lives of those who would be beautiful
again, they gather to push the numbing petals

in their blood. Pale as angels, they press
their bodies from their bodies, and so from us.

And a part of us grows more tender, sore,
looking for the viable vein to enter.

Those who would be starlets once again,
they stiffen their faces with Botox and pins,

as if the only way out were in, the only
vocation of beauty a love for the body

that throws the flesh away, longing to be
chosen, taken, seen. A great cloud beats

its breakers to shore, and the water rises,
and the narcissist leans into the glass

because he wants a way out, through the face
he never loved. No. Never sacrificed.

Never tore from the inner life it smothered.
It could be ours, this life, this flesh, this mirror.

Or the grave of someone he never heard
'til now, some fever or call he did not heed.

It could be blindness too, the way he lays
down there the belladonna of his body.

Go out and multiply, say the breezes.
Go out, says the candle. The suicidal bee.

Ventriloquist

It started with a doll, a woman,
who could have been his child and was
when, at times, his voice grew small
to go the places he could not go
alone. And like a child, the doll
had a hand for a heart that made her,
by charm of distant instinct, say
the things she never meant to say.
Nor did he for that matter,
whose arm vanished in her back
as if reaching through a mirror
or the sapwood of an old tree
to find the god transfigured there.
It was only a matter of time,
the day he would throw his voice
like a coin in a fountain
and lose it to the wish he made.
The gods would see to that, they
who know how a wish begins
with a hole in the body,
a burning question that has no answer,
but still you ask it, still you
breath it into the leafy voices
of the trees, dead and alive,
as if they were the earth that made them
speak and yours to give away.

Hands

And weary of the long day at work,
he takes off his hands and lays them

like a belt of tools at his bedside.
Naturally the first one proves

easier to remove than the second,
but the mouth serves as a third hand

as it often does in times like this.
And as he lies with nothing to do

but think about the things he is
not doing, his hands crawl away

out the pet door into a yard
dark with stars and the howling moon.

Such, of course is the nature
of hands, to point at this star

and that, and in their pointing stitch
the stars together, piece the bodies

of gods who, like hands, would make
the world into a world they love.

Truth is, there would be no gods
if these lights had not been torn

from one another. Mother from child,
child from the child he was.

Always a body back there,
somewhere, a ghost that slipped its coat

from the armature of bone.
Sirens slit the chest of silence,

and dogs pour through with mating calls
or calls of warning. Hard to tell.

Say they are one call, that they turn
to the mirrors of each other,

like palms, and touch, shade to shade.
When a man wakes, disheveled at dawn,

he understands: sleep is work
that never quite begins or ends,

but calls the sirens of the dogs
together: the world is too damn far

from the world; words far from words
and the animals that made them.

Still there is a tenderness
to the questions answers long for,

a one-eyed star of joy that fades
so we who wake might dream of it.

It's up there. In there. I see it. These hands
like doves on the arms of day.

The Ghost in the Shape of an Unnamed Flower

When Eduard Hitzig wired a living brain
and found a shock here raised an arm, there

a finger, he made a map and planted the flags
of native German into the strange new world.

If you are wondering what place does what,
come. Sit. The region that raises your hand

is the chair where the scientist is busy
shocking your brain. And his brain is shocked

in turn by the guy in the chair in his head,
the seeker you cannot see. No one does.

If you are like me, you are always in
the way. The old gods of the wind have little

on those of the blind heart beating in panic.
The anthropologist living with the natives

can empathize. He knows what it is like
to study the behavior of a tribe with some

anthropologist in it. What is a point
of view, asks the cortex. Where does it start.

And why does a shock in the pre-frontal
portion do nothing. Or nothing we observe.

Only a flash on a scan that could be someone
stranded in the dark. It could be Eduard,

now that we know him a little better,
and he knows us. It could be his research

agenda among the nocturnal flowers
where he snaps off his flashlight and lies down

weary with the scent. And though he cannot
see them, they see him, and like the grave

he crawled from, he opens his mouth a bit
wider the deeper he breathes. And breathe he must

as the red leaves breathe. And then sleep.
And the flames in thousands come tumbling in.

Black Vinyl

When a dendrite fires it is,
for a time, quick to fire again.
In this way people were invented,
their capacity for boredom
and friends and all things good
or feared. Temptation makes
knowledge a habit, our minds lost
within our minds, and still we take
quiet pleasure in the patterns
of the near forgotten, the songs
we hum long before we know
that we are humming. Take the dead
friend you think about once,
twice a day, perhaps, and then
less and less. He is in there,
his face sketched in smoke
and music, his spirit going in
one ear and out as another.
And when the song is over,
you get that dim suspicion
it is your hand in there that picks
up the record needle, cautious,
the way love is rarely at first.
Your hand that shakes a little, as if
afraid of the crackle, the flame,
the burden you lay back down
in the long black groove, again.

Blindsight

No one can explain it,
how the blind eye sees
light the seer cannot,
the flicker in the distance
he points to dead on
thinking he is guessing.
This is not a dream,
he tells his damaged brain,
not a house in flames.
I have dreams that say
the same, and revenants
who see the things in me
daylight cannot fathom.
Bad news knocks the door
in its policeman's blue,
and the mother goes deaf.
She becomes two mothers.
Morning sky ignites,
and her pupils widen.
This is how panic looks
when it lays its black
coin against the eye.
Sometimes when I read
the paper I read aloud
for no one else to hear.
I barely notice, scanning
the obits, grieving
faintly for the small print
of those I meet there.

What I do know is this.
The sky is full of needles
and thread and the space
of wounds that never close.
We are going to need
more wires, says the maker
of brains who is dreaming
one day he will see
a dead thing dream of him.
Look at complexity all
you like and you are looking
through the invisible
part that sees. Why is it
the ear can always pick
out two names that carry
across a cocktail party.
Yours and death's. You hear
something of the whole
entanglement before you
know that you are listening.
It is too late to pretend
you are your experience.
All deaths are your death
now, just beneath the din
and chatter, the machinery
of bodies; beneath your name
that came from somewhere
out there, somewhere near,
and must be yours alone.

The Birth of the X-Ray

It might as well be bone, this wedding ring.
The way it haloes the finger, white on white,

that belonged to the wife of the inventor.
Or should I say, *explorer*, for he exhumed

a wilderness, and though people called
the new rays by his name, *Röntgren Rays,*

he christened them *X*, as in Madam X,
whose hieroglyph suggests a headless body

or some such variant in its equation:
the poison, the treasure, the error, the taboo.

X as in the point of impact, the boxer
clocked, the belfry knocked unconscious

at funerals and weddings. What do bells know.
It could be both at once for all they care.

The finger in the finger could be a bride
whose halo cannot touch her. Halos float.

They must. Such is their unbridled nature:
to be the gold that blossoms through the crown,

the phantom bell that says, one, one, one.
X as in ecstatic. Which we might be,

times like this, when the unknowable
lays us bare as sleep and weddings do,

and screen doors blown open in the wind.
Make no mistake. This is no funeral.

Joy writes its own invitation to being
the way gods do, and still they are concealed.

The veil rises, and then a seizure of light.
Who has not gone blind for the camera.

Or made believe the moment they are touched,
something's in their eye. And no one sees.

What the Prosthesis Says to the Missing Leg

We are creatures of envy, you and I,
you for the living, me for the once alive.

Not that you have vanished entirely
or that you continue. Just look at me.

Here in the angel spaces of your skin,
made useful there. I am not alone.

I slip into the sleeve of your memory
the way a new ship slips into the sea.

Mornings shatter something when they break.
Fish rise from the fathoms, and the black

beaches find them. The invisible
is everywhere. Once it was more simple.

In the beginning, there was no beginning.
That came later. Remember. There is no thing

more burdensome than the blood we let
fall deeper in debt. But you knew that.

You know the heart is a heavy object,
the smaller the heavier, old with neglect,

cold as light across the widowed moon.
You will always be first. The ghost white cane.

You who lead the body through infection
to loss, to the loss of loss, to me, your son,

propped against a bed at night. Is that you,
sweet air I slash, I shoulder, I wander through.

Freaks

Last night I grew another arm,
a small one, mind you, boy-small,
and like a boy it tumbled out
the middle of my head, and I
told myself, relax, be patient,
be one part miracle, another
blunder, which is when a man
who looked like me walked in,
and we gazed at one another
without touching, and our arms
made gestures we could not see,
save in the mirror of each other.
Pointless gestures, I imagined,
like some tentacle in a tide
one part moon, another planet.
I am learning to be beautiful,
said the arm to the mirror. Then
out of one man sprung another,
and we were nine arms, a brain
in each, and then a room of men,
an ocean of anomalies,
and the moon kept pulling arms
and men from men, because it
just felt good to do the pulling
and be pulled in return. Down here
accidents are the fuel of nature,
the one god who trips and shatters
into many. You understand.
You were a god once, a child's

hand raised with all the answers,
and it took a lot of nightmares
to get this far, where you are learning
to be beautiful. The sea knows.
It is full of mistakes that make it
restless and uncertain. Ropes
of kelp like drowned boys that won't
go down. Children arrive each day
to horrified looks that angle
their heads and sweeten into worry.
Another night, another nightmare
plunging through the body, and we
are learning to be beautiful,
furious as waves that flood the eye.
For though the disfigured keep
moving into margins—first
the church steps, then the circus,
then the inner sanctum of sleep's
god-knows-where—they are out there.
They are learning to be older
and, like us, strangers to their faces,
apprenticed to the blood's dissolve,
where looking on might be mean
at first and then it's merciful,
and then, like beauty, more terrible
than cruel, it is no dream at all.

Spill

And when they lowered the casket, a boy,
inconspicuous one moment, camouflaged

in black, broke down in tears of laughter,
howling the whole measure of his breath,

becoming large with it, until the others,
shocked at first, realized it was serious,

for there would be no comforting the child
who could barely speak, let alone explain.

So he was led away, as grief continued
down the columns of the funeral program,

a song here, a memory, a prayer. Truth is,
a spell had broken: the little ones laughed

quietly here and there, and mothers felt
a strange incursion of wonder and worry.

Everywhere the hearts in mourning bloomed
a little like a startled flock of birds.

There is an empty region in the middle
of the brain, a ventricle, where the vessels

burst time to time. Who would have guessed
this was the time and the surge of blood

would fill the emptiness to overflowing.
No, it was not joy. Not the child's in question

who woke confused in his hospital bed.
He too grieved in the bewildered way

of boys whose serious suits never fit them,
whose prayers are unoriginal and old.

At the center of the brain is no one
a child knows, just a kid inside a kid

who likes to break things to see what's in them.
Inside a funeral is another funeral,

and inside that a blank space, a sky,
and somewhere in the distance a harp lies down

inside a piano and starts to praise
the shores of paradise it has no memory of.

Still we listen. We lie down with the sun
that has no cares—how calm as it sets

itself on fire. And there, the gulls who cackle,
not knowing what it the joke is, only

that they are hungry, it's heaven after all,
where happiness is infectious, where bodies

reach out to be recalled, and waves break
like bread as if that's the way to mend them.

Dusk spills its wine on the white carpet
and everyone pauses at the reception in awe

to watch it spread, the way laughter spreads
from cell to cell, and they forget what it was

they were saying, and they feel a small ache
open inside them and will not be consoled.

Manet

Can you blame a syphilitic
if he simplified his view
in the end, if he disavowed
the peripheral, his lilacs

one more window to the late
cabaret of his survival.
Call it blindness if you will,
the hope that would relegate

his ailment to some miracle.
If his withered foot turned black
or his fingers froze from lack
of blood, any wonder he called

on the lower angels. Gifts,
these last arrangements, from a friend
who is a still life now, framed
to give her body to his art,

to place inside the tiny coffin
of her iris another iris,
its stem cut, its petals bruised,
its ghost a scent the twilight opens.

The Anatomy Lesson

After Rembrandt

Why they look away is anyone's guess,
these men apprenticed to the evidence,

gathered at the corpse the dark context
makes bright inside the surgical forum.

Anyone's guess why, at this instant,
even the teacher looks past his subject,

the harp strings of these extended tendons
raised up from the bed of the open wound.

A spectacle, it seems, for no one there,
for though they lean in, wide-eyed, severe,

they look instead at the anatomy volume
propped up in the center of the room,

or at us, the viewer, the painter, the future
that stares back with the blindness of a mirror.

If it's true, they look down now and then,
it is never when we are looking at them,

transfixed by the painter's eye, long deceased,
whose gaze touches everything we see.

It frees us, to see a thing as being seen,
to understand it more, and less, as science

in its mercy would put aside our grief.
Not just what we feel for the man himself,

The painter knows. The corpse is a stranger,
a thief, fresh from the executioner's floor.

And yet, if you look close at the navel,
you will see the painter's faint initial,

the dark *R* curled into the silent chamber.
Call it pride, wit, the embalming fluid of art.

Call it reclamation. Whatever the reason,
an artist lies inside it, inside the criminal

who, for all we know, broke down with none
to see him at the gallows, to speak his name.

III.

Sacrum

You, my cobra, my spear-flint, my blade,
my hard white valentine thrust downward

into darkness, what is a body without
your little spade at the bottom, the seat

of the soul, as the Greeks would have it,
what but an arrogant tower in collapse.

Any wonder we wince now and then,
having met you, cursed you, turned away

like a flock of birds startled by a question.
To every soul, an underworld it charms

its passage in and out. You, my lyre,
my thermometer rising, hello down there,

my sacred bone, the one the ancients cut
from the sacrifice to lay at the altar.

Who would not cultivate the black soil
you turn, and, as bodies will, plant a seed.

And out of that: a tree, a flag, a city,
glass walls and carillons to climb the air.

But let us not get ahead of ourselves,
like the man glued to his computer

whose neck is killing him, or the manic
voice in the choir, or the anxious gait

that pulls the broker's head toward some breakdown
in the system. You were always there

to tug the brain by its enormous root,
not out of virtue or pleasure, but some other

appetite, like joy, that feeds the host.
For isn't it a bit fictitious, the soul

as merely personal, when the flight
from it is more so. Let us not get ahead

of the child's cry that brought us here,
apart from the others, to become a gift.

Hello down there, says the woman who offers
the cradle of her body to another, in love,

in hunger, or both. You were never one
to make clear, save the ways that hunger does.

Hello down there, says the churchyard shovel,
and the apple blossoms blush in answer.

Soliloquy of a Tornado in the Distance

I knew a girl once
who threw her breakables
at the dorm room wall
and cursed her redhead
lover in a strange tongue,
and all my friends at college
said, hell, she is Greek,
and he Irish, which meant
we understood nothing
of the glasswork that is
a human heart, the way
it glistens like the spit
in the screams of *yes*
that sexed the night to come.

And yes, it made us
envious, if bemused,
and no less sympathetic
with dread, to hear them
pound their affirmations
all the way in and then,
to spite us, farther in.
Attached at the places
they rubbed raw, they felt
the grip of something
which had as little to do
with each other, and us,
as wind with its sirens,
hammer with its nail.

Last night I dreamed of girls
in chairs at the dark edge
of the dance floor, and their
shyness made me shy,
a stranger in my skin,
and I turned from them
to the apple blossoms
in the window, the street-
walker scent of April
rising. And in the distance,
more lovely still, more
fierce in its skirt of trash:
a great tornado, dark arms
flailing, drawn this way.

So this is how a monk feels
on the mountain path
in a Japanese print,
only the parchment is on
fire. And terror the new
sublimity that scales you
down. The supplicant
becomes one small part
of the scene. The rest
the you that is not you,
just as disaster is not
a dream for the dreamer.

I was a new girl once
I never knew at all.

I sat in my dark chair
as the winds blew our windows
out, like candles, all
at once, and the blouses
shuddered. I see you,
said the wind in the strange
tongue of broken things,
the only tongue it knows.
I came before you
and so continue. And so
I understand nothing
of sacrifice and rage
and wicks that understand
nothing of the flame.

Hard to be sentimental
about a wind and be
the one you are. Why else
do you wake disheveled.
I knew a girl once
whose tirades got me off
and then, well, they got
a little boring. Move,
said the wind, and the hearts

of the wilderness seized,
listening. And then they heard
nothing. Only stillness.
And then they beat a little
faster. And faster still.

Ocean

Wind, when it comes, comes in waves,
and we call it one *wind*, though it is many,

and we hear in it the others that fall
into the desert with the sound of falling.

Times when I tell myself I am here,
I am already thinking of another place,

as one thinks of a man and no sooner
what that man means or does not mean

now that he is gone. Call this the land
of winds. Far from the sea I came from,

the tide that nearly killed me as a child.
Far too from the child and his panic

that rose and fell for decades in my sleep,
as I too fell, whenever I felt small.

The sea was beautiful then, the monstrous swells
that battered me like a flag in the wind.

But it was no monster. No mother either.
I survived it. And when I found my father

he did not believe me or know what to say.
He was not cruel. He was a hard worker

who, like any ocean, spoke the language
he knew and gave more gifts than explanations.

I do not know if my father paused
before the giant waves in awe sometimes,

if, when he was young, the great sea
below his warship spoke to him at all.

I know only it was a sea we looked at
when, in the end, we talked to one another

at the water's edge, him with his damaged
English, me pretending to understand.

Sunlight burned a hole in the horizon.
And in my confusion, I felt the odd

affinity of not knowing, the way one feels
closer to the sea the moment you give it

space, silence, terror even, things no sea
mends or masters in its thrashing arms.

Harvest of the Willows

Say you are hung by one
pin in nothing but air
and barely touching down,
that you are the broom
that sweeps the leaves you shed,
so there is always something
more to your vocation,
something unaccomplished
in your look of battered
drunkenness, something
sweet that walks and walks
the cold indifferent stream.
Always more of you
to clear the mirror you,
unthinking, clear again.
Small wonder a painter
laid a drowned girl there,
in the unburdening
drizzle of leaves that eat
their shadows as they fall.
Her gown is your gown now,
woven with your branches,
your loose-limbed cotton
that withholds the breast
it offers in return. Oh,
I know. You get that a lot,
you flexing for the lens
smeared in an unction
of discouragement and pity,

styled just so. In truth,
you are no harp, no starlet.
I heard you sing as much.
The wind in you is far too
invisible and large.
And though you reach down
to touch the girl in us,
she is a stranger still,
as beauty is, and must be
to be beautiful. She
and the difficult ones
we never listened to
enough, the drunk friend,
the mind with voices, the long
scared and willowy
body that laid its muscles
here beneath the silver
of a day that could be
most any day, scattered
without grief or mercy
to these, our sleeping faces.

The Tadpoles

Just this morning I felt the last ripple
and chill of their vanishing parts,

their weird small feet as they swam away,
back into the swampland, into the boy

I was when I first laid eyes on one—
so small in my father's hand it made

that hand a little larger, more dangerous,
more the father, mindful as he cupped

his dreary soup to float the writhing arms.
A spectacle too brief, too half-remembered:

the slit of the open eye, the slime-smooth
effluvial tail before the flesh would take it.

And so I woke that night and lit a branch
in the coals of the fire-circle by my tent

to walk the path to the water-line alone.
It was the dry season, and every torch

a bad idea. Everywhere the crackle
of the brush that withered into blossom.

More than any campfire and its story,
the tadpoles held me, their language verging

on a language, or so the silence said.

Every day I wash my face in silence,
the frog in me released to swim the mirror.

I look more and more the father as I go.
I understand what it is to worry

about a child who crawls from his tent
at night, who goes searching for a stick.

I want to promise him we will return
in the morning, though, truth is, it will be

different. He will be water in my hand.
I will drink my tea and swallow the foul

angelic flesh of dreams I cannot recall.
Just some vague shivery kinship that says,

wonder is hazard; the death of wonder
more hazardous still. Ask the boy I was—

he is older than me—ask him as he kneels
to coil the sleepy writher in his hand,

is there a frog there still, a child's child,
a midnight chirping. How terribly odd, this hand.

The Narrow Roads of Winter

My mother's operation was a light snow
that turned her hair white, her pallor cold,
her hand to the shivering thing in the air

that pleaded, stay, no, stay, and I did,
the way a child stays waiting for a ride
in winter, as night falls like a bridal veil.

And yes it saved her, the long vessel slit
from her leg, planted in her chest, to feed
the muscle. A body eats itself to survive.

I get that. Winter takes in the blood
and wafer of a near forgotten season,
and still it is winter. That's the hard part:

the bone-white ice of hands that held me,
the will to walk broken long before her legs
gave out, the talk that resolved to one song,

one note, one quiet shroud that fell across
the eye at night, where all in time grew
cruel, still, insistent, stupefied in snow.

Summons

Behind each face is another.
It has the name the body

bears, but it has no body.
It persists. Face after face

falling from its template,
its phantom mold we never see.

I am thinking of a friend
whose mother lost so much

history and blood, I wonder,
is death one thing, or many,

more near than believed,
when we were young.

If it bears the unseen face
of a woman, however damaged,

across one threshold,
what of the angel of the new,

the odd will to be new,
part of us we have no claim to.

Tonight I hear a nursing home
fill with the breath of an only ocean.

I hear the space of the ocean
inhale the air in the branches

of our lungs. And my question
suddenly has less to do

with where we are going than how.
What would we let go,

what child who runs ahead in darkness.
Have we rehearsed our death

to death, hands emptied into other
hands, laughter into laughter.

What face dissolves and with it
the summons to everything

we were not, the turbulence
that made our lives hell and full

of mercy, the kind we hear still.
The pleats of skirts and falling

waves, the strange new hush
inside the mother. It is in there,

The day a mother's face first
brightened ours. And we will never

quite remember. Day after day
fading from the template of one

ghost day. When we were young.
And death was far away.

The Invention of Clouds

The clouds will eat most anything these days.
A home, a hand, a mirror, the human face
of every scaffold and tower in the haze.
Cloud swallows cloud who must go nameless.

Any wonder we rise from the open
grasses of the plains, to find ourselves
among them, one part earth, another wind.
The monuments know what it is to live

enthralled inside the fog that blinds them,
not seeing the skies in light of being one.
If you are what you eat, do you become
in turn what eats at you. The steeple pins

its hopes to what: the occasional cloud
it cuts to glimpse inside. What is a past
but everywhere and lost, a living shroud,
that, in another light, could be the mist

of some chrysalis. World begets world
the way the fly begets the frog, the last
the lasting, and on it goes, our thunder spilled
like morning's face into the looking glass.

Sometimes when I search for lost friends,
they are so many clouds, buckets of light
pouring through the river. Which understands
less than it accepts. Like us. Effacement

is the new paradise, the water that bears
heaven on its shoulders, a thing so large
it weighs nothing, or nothing that is ours.
Who has not been a body on the verge

of breaking down, or open, in pleasure
or pain, or both at once, to see your eye
drown in the eye it sees, the vague contours
of its planet plunged through another sky.

What we want terrifies. Cloud begets cloud
that in turn would vanish on our lips
if not for the need to breathe. The winds
move, and so push along the little ships

of leaves in the current, bound for shores
of some otherworld, bearing in their hold
a small request, that they are never more
for being less, just one among the cold,

cumulous flocks led each night to slaughter.
Yes, you could see them that way, or called
downstream to pasture, cloud after cloud
rolled open in the mirror. Like a door.

Water Burial

No end to the river's rituals
of passage, the ablutions of believers
knee-deep in the green

scent and glacial runoff of the Ganges,
the cool connective tissue of a people
washing down their backs.

What is a body if not a thing of water,
what a river if not a pilgrim who wanders
south to the open sea.

Monks come and go as tributaries do
whose names remain behind them as they pass,
and we look to the boat

ablaze against the slate of the surface,
against the mirrored image where it floats.
We look to the ripple

of the sail and the glare that pulls it,
to the stench and the glory, the russet
current fouled with soot,

hung from heaven by a braid of smoke.
We look to the man on fire who is two
men now, one who rises,

one who sinks: in time they separate.
In time we look because we cannot look
away, clothed in white

as is the custom. These boats go somewhere.
Stars feed the crematorium of dawn.
These still horizons call

to someone, something, a name we were given,
a song we heard, though where, we cannot say,
only a tiny ember

now and then, here a melody, there a word.

Metaphysics of the Literal Heart

There is no beyond except

In the mind, which is
It turns out the body after all

Where we live, whole-

Hearted. Where surface will not hold
We must shatter.
—Katherine Coles

Or this: the skin gives a little,
it breathes, it must, so that we might

not shatter. We allow room
for the motions that sustain us,

for the body ghosted by a will
we know so little about. Still

we choose. Still we know enough
to make our choices matter

and so revise them. I know a girl
who has a tattoo of the earth

between the wings of her scapulae.
They make of her an angel

of that world that flies a little,
needled into the literal blood below.

*

When she lies on her stomach,
eyes to her pillow, the planet flutters

into the night sky behind her.
The moon there fueled with sticks

gathered from the day before.
When she lies on her back,

she looks up through closed eyelids
at stars that have not been invented.

*

Earth falls to earth like a coin in a well.
Some nights the heart is that coin,

falling forever without a splash.
It is down there somewhere, the wish

you made like a chair or a theory.
Let us call it a thing. Let us be clear.

If there is an earth on your skin,
it breathes to exchange what it must,

holds in some measure of the freedom
to choose. It survives the way

the name of a river survives the river,
rusted with silt in the rainy season.

*

The skin boxes up the literal heart
like a gift. To live is to hide something,

to be specific and so a species, an earth
winged in the dark between the stars.

On a good day, the earth is breathing
with wells. But where it grips, it splits.

It breaks down like a widow at the knees.
(I know a girl with a planet on her back.)

And then the falling dust, so slow
it feels like stillness coming down.

(I know a girl who dreams of flying.)
Somewhere a movement in the rubble.

(Whose dream of flying says she cannot.)
Somewhere the cry of a distant siren.

*

Sure, there are worlds that hold to their surface,
so far as we know, that do not fracture.

There are dead planets that grieve no one,
whose nights clamp shut the desert sand.

They hang sharp in the air like jewels.
There are those who do not believe

in a buried life. They are aware of forms.
But there are no forms of awareness.

There cannot be. Planets come and go.
And yes, as we say, we are aware.

*

True. Some people buy a little time
with another man's heart inside them.

They briefly die on the operating table.
They leave the room to the moment,

their body to the world. In time
their chests close to swallow the wafer.

And when they wake, they hear voices
in the hall, the beeps of the machinery.

And everything seems too strange
to be strange exactly. That comes later.

And they feel too alone with this to feel
alone. That comes later. Or not at all.

*

If I pinned a planet to my back,
it would be to honor where I came from,

to see it from a distance, small and thus entire,
like a sand dollar the night washed in.

It would be to hold that distance,
the way love for a girl would hold her image.

She who is no earth but of it, her mind
no body and nowhere without it.

Tempting, to simplify a world, our world,
to what we say about it. As if the thing

we held articulated just how we hold it.
One thing is certain: the mind is no body.

*

If it were, the say-so would be dead.
Without conflict, curiosity, faith.

Today I read of violence in the temple.
I nearly forgot where I was. And then

music fell through the neighbor's branches
like evidence. It walked me through the rest.

When a man dies, the others close his eyes.
They pull a cloth across his face.

They talk to him through the surfaces
of words. Each in his aloneness talks

to something. And then they bury him,
back to the earth, face to the absent stars.

*

I have a friend who believed in names
as bodies, in bodies as surfaces,

in surfaces as the limits of the world.
He died of drink from the insides out.

When I sat with him at the clinic,
waiting for the scope's results, he shivered

like water. Why always dust to dust,
never water to water. Never the self he theorized

as no self, or the theory as disavowal
of theories. Only a watery assemblage

of surfaces, norms, rebellions, economies,
pleasures. Do not believe what you hear.

*

Theories are practical. Like guns. Like bread.
They commit their acts in the still arms

of a chair or stranger or harbor after dark.
They are practical in the way they make us

do the things we never think to do.
I too love them: the ache of the river

for the open sea. A world longs to hold
a world, and so be held, seen after, made new.

A theory longs to sit by the ocean
where the shush of erasure gets more monstrous

like an internet, or history, or God's love
that spins the haloes of the particles.

*

So when it was time, when the doctor told my friend
what she could not see, how the damage

was such she could not feed the scope past
the scarring at the bottom, I thought, a man

like that knows a hunger I cannot fathom.
And between his hunger and him

a theory that went just so far, no farther.
He once told me he forgot two years

of his childhood, just a big blank,
no map, no edge, no form. For all we know,

it did not exist. Just a hole at the bottom
of the chamber where the waters flow.

And he was free, he thought, to look
at nothing. Or not look. What did it matter.

*

Let us bracket off those monsters
on old maps, the ones that tell us

something we cannot know. Let us
sail to the edge of the world

which we cannot see as such.
Who made this map anyway.

Let us sail to the brink of disaster
and sail no more, because the world

will not hold itself as a world
unless we come about. Let us drink.

Burn the margins of our experience.
Monsters, hell, I'll show you monsters.

*

The mapping mind holds its compass
in its eye like a monocle. It holds us

in bounds, on course, or else we break.
Or is it the map that breaks.

To wake in the night frightens
a little light from the bottom of the ocean.

Ask that heart where it beats
the door of the visible world.

Is not the dream of the unified field
a bit of mind over the matters of experience.

One thing is certain: a body is not a body
alone, unless, perhaps, it's dead.

*

Ask the circle if it is a closed
or open thing, a cup, a throat,

a mouth of darkness as we sleep.
This ocean grows heavy as we breathe it,

the way a lost memory of abuse
grows heavy in the arms of the abused.

I understand. How do we know
what we say until we say it.

See there, the insistence:
the implied giver, the strange receiver,

the strange new thing
no word has ever said.

*

Words see into words
the way a mother sees into a distant child.

She cannot create the one she names.
When he crowns, he wounds.

When he cries, her heart beats
a deeper path. And it goes on that way:

the howl, the worry, the waking
in the night. In her sleep,

gathering waves of blood that shatter
to be heard.

Acknowledgments

The author would like to thank the following journals in which these poems first appeared:

Birmingham Poetry Review, Blackbird, BODY, Cutthroat, Descant, Epoch, Fiddlehead, The Florida Review, The Gettysburg Review, The Laurel Review, IN Quire, Interim, The Journal, The Kenyon Review, Linebreak, Measure, Missouri Review, New England Review, The New Ohio Review, OmniVerse, Plume, Poetry Northwest, Queen's Quarterly, Raritan, Stand, The Yale Review, and *Zone 3*

The poem "The Invention of Clouds" also appeared in *Ley Lines* (Wilfrid University Press).

Bruce Bond is the author of sixteen books including *For the Lost Cathedral* (Louisiana State University Press, 2015), *The Other Sky* (Etruscan Press, 2015), *Immanent Distance: Poetry and the Metaphysics of the Near at Hand* (University of Michigan Press, 2015), *Gold Bee* (Crab Orchard Award, Southern Illinois University Press, 2016), and *Black Anthem* (Tampa Review Prize, University of Tampa Press, 2016). He has received numerous honors including the Allen Tate Award, the New South Award, the Knightville Poetry Award, the Richard Peterson Prize, and fellowships from the National Endowment for the Arts and the Texas Commission on the Arts. Presently he is Regents Professor at University of North Texas.

Publication of this book was made possible by grants and donations. We are also grateful to those individuals who participated in our 2016 Build a Book Program. They are:

Anonymous (8), Evan Archer, Sally Ball, Jan Bender-Zanoni, Zeke Berman, Kristina Bicher, Carol Blum, Lee Briccetti, Deirdre Brill, Anthony Cappo, Carla & Steven Carlson, Maxwell Dana, Machi Davis, Monica Ferrell, Martha Webster & Robert Fuentes, Dorothy Goldman, Lauri Grossman, Steven Haas, Mary Heilner, Henry Israeli, Christopher Kempf, David Lee, Jen Levitt, Howard Levy, Owen Lewis, Paul Lisicky, Katie Longofono, Cynthia Lowen, Louise Mathias, Nathan McClain, Gregory McDonald, Britt Melewski, Kamilah Moon, Carolyn Murdoch, Tracey Orick, Zachary Pace, Gregory Pardlo, Allyson Paty, Marcia & Chris Pelletiere, Eileen Pollack, Barbara Preminger, Kevin Prufer, Peter & Jill Schireson, Roni & Richard Schotter, Soraya Shalforoosh, Peggy Shinner, James Snyder & Krista Fragos, Megan Staffel, Marjorie & Lew Tesser, Susan Walton, Calvin Wei, Abigail Wender, Allison Benis White, and Monica Youn.